Mixtape of the Unsaid

Mixtape of the Unsaid

By JS Belote

Mixtape of the Unsaid
Copyright ©2014 JS Belote.
All rights reserved.

No part of this book may be performed, recorded or otherwise transmitted without the written consent of the author and the publisher. However portions of the poems may be cited for book reviews without obtaining such consent.

Printed in the United States of America
First Edition February 2014
ISBN 978-0-9910904-0-2

Published by Edwin E. Smith Publishing
edwinesmith.com
199 Clark Road, McRae, Arkansas 72102

Welcome to Edwin E. Smith Publishing's Emerging Authors Series. This series will offer works of prose or poetry by authors who are underrepresented in publication. We hope this series will assist in creating appropriate recognition of their talents.

JS Belote's ***Mixtape of the Unsaid*** is the first title to be presented in Edwin E. Smith Publishing's Emerging Authors Series.

Contents

The gleaming kind

Why the dumb don't speak	3
He might turn up working odd jobs at your favorite diner	5
Digging a grave	7
Eating clams	10
The doldrums	11
Self-portrait as dark green orange rot	13
The red dress	15
In the end	16
Trout fishing	17
A moon & blue crabs	18
Like a thief unhinging himself from his shadow	20
Utter	22

Before then there was no answer like the dead   25

Beyond the center: an essay on the creative process   35

The gleaming kind

Why the dumb don't speak

like the cow tongue
strung up in the slaughterhouse
in my dream I stared at it
hoping it would talk tell me
about God I thought but
it didn't even tremble
on the hook didn't even
stir the cold soup I licked
from your lips when
your breath came heavy
while you slept you would
whisper too sometimes not words
but murmurs from somewhere
deep you sounded old like
distant thunder or the thunder
of horses painted
on cave walls I would lean in closer
turn my head so my ear grew
damp & warm with you & think
tell me about God
I'm ready to hear
the whole word now but you never
spoke I'd tell you
as a child I'd try to notice
the moment I'd fall asleep
but never could it'd escape
like a cave mouth
& what's hidden in it
in the dark I'd wake
in the morning forget my dreams
by noon & try again that night
now I wake sometimes when it's still
dark my tongue heavy afraid
I can't breathe gasping for all

Mixtape of the Unsaid

that air between you
& me warm & awful left behind
by thunder a lion licking the heart
of a dead horse in the settling dust
& original wind.

He might turn up working odd jobs at your favorite diner
After Frank Stanford

where my father & I are eating omelets
& drinking coffee spreading grape jelly
too thin onto burnt toast we didn't ask for

dirty windows with handprints obscure
the city the nameless faces the happy

& sad he tells me when he was a kid
he'd trace the design of oblong shapes on tabletops
like this one & try to find

where the pattern repeated

I tell him I liked to breathe on glass & mirrors
& draw odd symbols in them because
when the fog faded they'd be hidden until

someone breathed there again & had to wait

for their face to reappear through its fading
so they could finish putting their makeup on
I hoped it made them wonder

He tells me the eggs here are good
but the coffee is weak I notice the booth seat

beside me is worn a bit so the foam blooms
from it like an ugly flower from a grave

or the fake smile from the cook who scrapes
the stovetop clean & wipes the dirt from his hands

on his apron & fills a bucket up
with water to mop when he leaves he walks out

with his boot soles wet & you can follow him
a trail of dark hexes repeating down

the street to the pond where they vanish
just a few boats with men in them

fishing putting hooks in worms
& sometimes their fingers.

Digging a grave

Someday with the sleep
of a shovel in his hands & the knees
of his blue jeans worn
white he'll turn to ask you why
you're hiding by the barn door you'll say

galloping horses from your tongue
into the dark
& pick up the heavy can for gasoline
filled with water & drink to put
the fire in your belly out

he'll go on digging the grave
in the garden for his dog

wiping the sweat from his forehead
with a red handkerchief the motion
almost as old as death itself

he'll ask you where you've been
before this & if you say
the store to buy fish for dinner
he'll nod & point at the grave

wait for you to put the dog in it

you should cook it with butter he'll say
so it glistens against the black pan like a woman
standing alone at night sweating
in a white gown

you always thought of her
in red though

Mixtape of the Unsaid

at the sink cleaning off
the knives with merlot on her lips
& sex hair the window next to her lit

orange by a streetlamp

you always thought of how she stopped
when the bad pop songs came on
to dance with the knives
over her head how she cut
your reflection into them

you thought you loved her for it

when you took her on the kitchen table
her eyes were dark & wild & the same

as the white horse you led back
to the burned down barn as a child
with an apple & you thought
you loved her…

when she left palm prints on the bed sheets
the dog licked at them

when the streetlamp went out

the window went dark
like someone was shoveling
dirt on it the dark lines under
their fingernails smiling
their hands white like yours
but whittled by death
their face…

JS Belote

when the grave is done

he'll turn to you again
but not say anything

you'll know it's time.

Eating clams

At low tide we'd go
down to the beach with old
trowels all rusty & buckets
& dig up clams. A trick was
to toss big rocks
& watch for spurts
of water from the mud
& run over & start
digging. If you were
quick enough you could
get lots of clams. Then
you could put them
in boiling water, they
don't scream like
lobsters do, then you
could eat them
with melted butter
I always burned my tongue.

JS Belote

The doldrums

In those days I thought death
was a dog that wouldn't stop
licking itself under the table

that would rest its head on my boots
so I couldn't move them
while I whittled soap
into trout

I thought it was an old woman
I had to
spoon-feed slow-cook oatmeal
& buttermilk because her fingers

were like dead snakes

her smile a clothesline weighed down
with wet jeans

& her stories all about the dust

after that I thought death was a bad joke
that started in a pool hall
after too many drinks

& soon everyone was telling it a boy in the woods
in the snow

my friend's mother at night
in the backseat of her car
the parking lot unlit
by the school

she didn't leave a note

Mixtape of the Unsaid

rolled up in the empty bottle of pills
like I would I said then
like my body was

a dark ship in the doldrums

like I'd spent time trying to discuss
Nietzsche with the fish & seagulls

studying the clouds

If it was a joke I said
I'd want some humor in it

but now I think it's a dog again
a stray I found out back
starving by the garbage
its ribs like thin fingers

because even though I fattened it up
& put a collar on it
it still doesn't listen to me
I call its name all night sometimes

but it stays by the door between the bedroom
& the hallway its eyes yellow & hollow
always looking at me & hardly breathing.

Self-portrait as dark green orange rot

1

I bought an orange
chair at the antique market. Corduroy & the color
of my grandparent's basement. Also, I always scratch
mosquito bites until they open.
Then they scab—yellow, which is
not the color I hoped for (it's hard to stare
at the sun for long enough to see it)—& I'll pick it off later.

2

When the sky bruises
bats fly out of the church roof. I watch
your face in all
the sepia ink fading in the photo
to see if it's still moving. I don't know
you, & your herringbone tweed
coat is the first thing
I drip wax on when it's dark when the power goes out from
snow.

3

Your face never moves though.
Your eyes are made of paper.
I don't know you.
I've heard there is a number that infinitely approaches zero.
The bats fly in wide circles, wildly. I don't know
you or anyone else in the photos I thumbed through (in the
shoebox
in the store on highway one)

4

wildly like when I was kid in the basement putting glue on
my fingers
& waiting for it to dry
so I could peel it off (like it was the body
& enough fervor could worry it back to the dark green
sky spreading over the oranges
in the fruit bowl upstairs)
& see the design of my fingerprints.

The red dress

is all I have now.
I won't go back to that room,
to the white sill with two apricots
cut down their centers
& into their shadows. Of light,
I've overused it,
of the red dress,
it's gone now already,
of what metaphors I have left to wring out
the rest of you with—
sawdust kicked to the side
by whoever cares enough, a little moonlight
pooled on the workbench—are too ignorable
to burn. Smoke rising in the sky
from a relit cigarette. A doorway to a brick wall
because, here in Richmond, the abandoned homes
are boarded up
or broken into,
the old factories, refurbished
& turned into cheap lofts.
Every branch I toss in the river
& throw stones at
is like drinking the warmest soda
we left it in the car all day at the beach.
If this is a mixtape
of the unsaid, & the shadow on the page
is my hand, then the ink marks are geese
I watch for a moment with the stone still
in my palm, the unimaginable north behind them,
the unimaginable south before them,
get shot down by hunters.

In the end

This will mean what
dirt means when
the boot print in it
filled with mud
dries the color
of pig's blood

my mother scrubbed
from the pen fence
after the night an owl
swooped in & stole
four newborns. The sow

left the fifth for dead
& my step-father found it
blue in the morning.
My mother gave
The sixth goat's milk.
This will be confused

like the blood If you saw
all this from a distance
& wondered why
a woman would
work so hard to scrub
away dried mud & why

she kept using a dirty sleeve
to wipe the sweat
from under her eyes.

Trout fishing

She took the bone out
of her mouth.

There wasn't much
chicken left on it.

Her fingers were wet
with grease. She said do you want
some desert, grabbed a knife.

I said no. Do you want
more wine, her lips
stained with merlot.

I nodded. You need to suck
& bite your lips
to get the wine off

I said, but not enough
to make them bleed.

She poured my glass to the brim,
Giggling. She wasn't wearing
Anything. She looked silver

In the light like a trout
right before it bites a hook.

I touched her gently
like a wound.

A moon & blue crabs

Sometimes at night I go out
to the cut with a flashlight & wade
into the cold water

the current pulls at me
the ripples my legs
give out drift off in the tide

if the moon's full
I make a second moon

on the water the dark red
seaweed sways in it

sometimes the nightgown

I soaked in the sink once
to scrub wine from

is hung on the clothesline

it moves in the wind
when I look back like you're still
wearing it like you want me

to come over & touch your hip

your thigh your collarbone

but I won't
I tell myself it's not there

I wade farther in & wait
for the first blue crab to slink out

from the seaweed

I shine my light on it

I love how they freeze & gleam
fluorescent how they put

their claws up & open them

as if to praise
in a binding terror.

Like a thief unhinging himself from his shadow

I threw my dark shirt over the lamp to dim the room

dipped my fingers in ink & left
black whorls on the comforter

& bed sheets watched the worst t.v.

the light was colorful on the walls & old photos
of the people I didn't know

I'm not a thief but sometimes

I feel like one with skin this pale I could've

stole the moon from the pond
I floated in once on my back it was night

swallowing sounded so loud
when my ears filled with water so close

then owl calls brought the distance back

if I wanted to sink then to let water
fill my lungs with the unutterable

cold it was only for a moment
& harmless like my desire for sleep now

to be taken quietly into the unknown

but the t.v. is too bright
when I close my eyes the shapes of light linger

the hints of faces it's too bright

JS Belote

to sleep the bed sheets like water

I want to steal myself back

under dark & quiet with no

gleaming fish swimming by
to wake me.

Utter

I can't draw it in—

the sensation of an arm,
asleep as you wake

in the dark, the weight
sudden; how the hand, half open

in its absence, seems
to be waiting for something…

another hand, perhaps,
or a bowl of goat's milk

like the cold mud you pulled
yourself from to walk back

to the house, the shape
of your hand still

there by the goat hooves
& dung. It's instinct

& I can't draw it in—

the way the young goats
know to head butt the udder

to get more milk & so
head butt the bottle & plastic

nipple when we feed them,
their mouths frothing.

The way they imagine something
unending, even when

it's not. Even

when it's not you
making my arm go numb

as I sleep, it's me
waiting for the blood to come back

so I can smooth out
the absent imprint of your body.

Before then there
was no answer like the dead

1.

Before then there was nothing…

or, at least, that's how I remember
it. Stones arranged like a spine

in the sand by someone

who walked off flawlessly, not
looking back, a cold coin

in the sky falling again to their hand.

In the legend the gulls cry
with a kind of primordial
excitement, the pillar

of salt full
of regret. My tongue bruised

from saying the names you
wore like stone necklaces
over & over. My fingers were stained

by the orange I peeled
for you, they were bitter
when I tasted them, they changed

the way I spoke.

2.

Then dust shook out the window from a rug.

Pennies for the blind
man's cup—seventeen & three nickels

& the taste of all the hands
they've been in, mixed with tokens

in my pocket. The way you fingered
the grooved edge to know,

& how easy it is to leave
change when I drop it in public

in the subway. If I imagine
the music behind the woman beating the rug out

it's Beethoven, & the sky is yellow
for a moment. If I imagine

the woman…
I must not

imagine the woman, the orange chair beside her
perfect, & worn to

the whorled wood.

3.

There is a way

there is no way
to describe your lips

coming apart to meet

mine. The apples
brown on & no one

eats them
or throws them out. Fruit flies

in the summer
flew into your mouth

& we made sad jokes

about them: moths that wanted to be

pressed in a wet book, birds

that gave their broken imprints
to windows, the eternal

currency. We didn't really laugh.

4.

Was or is it could
the scuffed gold coin
the blind man pulled
from the fountain
stand for then:

what we give up
& go to, & give up again,
the sad moments
in between, the year & face
nearly worn off. This is

the finest death; the first
one; the one that whispers
in your ear still. Watch:
he hides it like I did, rubbing
his fingers over it until

it gleams in the dark.

5.

No way to say your name
without saying table we gutted

fish at, too. When we cut

the scales off
they taught us how
a sheen divides itself;

the lamp & your eyes
reflected on either side of

the dull blade I gave
my blood to; a warm ruby.

6.

answer the moon
when it swells up in your window
like the belly
of a drowned man.

Answer it when it asks why
you don't dance
on the dam anymore, why you run

through white grass at night
getting your boots wet,
why you keep two coins in your pocket
like dirty suns

for the precious dead. Answer it when

it's only the thin white smile
on your window. When it says

how the hell have you been?
Did you miss me? How many
fireflies did you kill

trying to put me in a jar?

7.

like the dead fish the moon
lights up on a dark rock,

the slow fungus that grows
over the oranges
in a bowl,

your red dress
on the bathroom floor,

I'll make a death mask out of
the mundane.
I'll cut each piece of you

from me like holes
into a paper snowflake

& run through the woods
naked to the place where
I caught frogs as a kid.

I'll listen to the mosquitos
sing.

I'll put a hook in my lip
& jump in the pond. I'll wait

for the snapping turtles.
It'll look like I'm dancing
under the water.

Beyond the center:
an essay on the creative process

Beyond the center: an essay on the creative process

The creative process is, for me, primarily, an act of opening, an act of allowing life to rise up from within me in its most nascent form, and an act of living into that life with a great intensity. It's an act of ordering an inner chaos that stems from the inability, existentially speaking, to truly understand the world around me or comprehend my *place* in it, and the sense of disconnect that comes from that tension. It is, essentially, an effort to reconcile and find solace in, the gap between the deep feeling of authentic *life* and the sense of inauthenticity that pervades living in a world that feels inexplicably separate from me. This solace only occurs during the creative process when a discovery of what sleeps dormant under the gauze of conscious thought is found. And so, because the conscious thought is given up in favor of intuition, the creative process is a kind of offering of the known (or preconceived) for the unknown, an alms of the certain for the uncertain, it is an enactment of the mystery of life, and so one begins to do as Rilke said and "live the questions." The question is: how does one do this?

To achieve some form of utterance, some accurate transcription of one's deepest emotional resonances onto a page in poem form, then one must not divorce the creative process from the experience of living. That is to say: the poet must live even more deeply while writing, must feel the ink in their veins, and hear the sound of each word echo in the cathedral of their skulls; one must experience while writing the very fabric from which life springs, the fabric we witness in our most honest expressions of joy, terror, sorrow, and so on. If this pure experience is not achieved during the creative process, and instead a kind of recollection and intellectualization of these moments is relied upon, then that separation will most certainly be evident in the poem. This is not to say a poem written in that manner cannot carry some merit, for craft can go a long way, but to say a poem written in that manner will lack the very gut of truth, experience, and emotion, because the very gut of those things can't be intellectualized.

It is therefore the task of the artist during the creative process to somehow transport themselves, both emotionally and experientially, into a moment, being, or object so that the poet is not composing the poem as an analytical outsider to the subject but as the subject itself, so that poet inhabits that place and time and writes with the blood of the animal or with the rain beating on the tin roof beating on the muscle of their heart, too. In this way the past and the future, the invalid and the alien, the mountain and the mole morph from mere imaginings to unadulterated and honest presence, and so transcription of that presence becomes possible. It is only through this honest presence a poem can access any deep truth.

What I am trying to say is that the creative process is not some kind of separation from or standing aside from life. It is the complete opposite; it is experiencing a moment of life so deeply and with such intensity that that moment is not only in the work of art but is the work of art. That is to say a work of art *is* a work of life. There is no other way for the nuances of experience to be truly present in a poem because all other methods rely upon a kind of analysis or logical progression of thought, which relies upon language in its most stale and dead form. To put it another way: language that is not moved by the deepest act of living, that is not lifted up by the most primordial life, relies upon and can only speak from its own self-referential system that is a product of life that has been already lived and not the present unbridling life itself. The difference is subtle but important. It is my feeling that the greatest poems were so lived into during the moment of composition that they gave birth to a new language or, perhaps more accurately, so transformed the language they were writing in with metaphor and symbolism that it became new. I imagine the process to be much like what the poet Li-Young Lee means when he describes art being a natural religion.

He offers the example of a volcano in Hawaii, how the fire and molten lava that spewed from the mouth has hardened into various shapes a few miles down the mountain. He compares dogmatic religion to a kind of worshipping of that hardened lava, a worshipping of godheads that had been created by people in the past during true religious experiences at the mouth of the volcano. The goal of the artist, he says, is stand again in front of the fire, to live at the source of life, and to create new godheads, new symbols for experience and existence. To return to my original point, this is why writing a poem through intellectualizing and conceptualizing an experience fails at a most fundamental level, because it relies upon the hardened symbols down the mountain. The poems I am interested in and interested in writing are ones that take place at, and bloom from, the mouth of the volcano. I want the very source of life to be what gives birth to the new symbols and metaphors; I want each poem to be its own kind of mythological system. In this way the creative act for the artist is an act of giving and creating life and so consequently parallels the greater creative force behind all life. It's in this way the creative process is almost an act of becoming a god.

However, achieving this moment in the creative process is not easy since it's a practice of entering into the unknown, and so the artist constantly faces, proceeds with, and lives into uncertainty. Since creation is inexplicably cuffed to absence in much the same way the light is cuffed to the dark, creation becomes a kind of dialogue with absence. What I mean by this is, practically speaking, during the creative process or, at least, the initial stages of the creative process, the artist must allow *life* to shape itself into the poem and so must stay entirely open to the experience without attempt to over analyze or intellectualize it. That is to say the artist must become a kind of void for life to rise out of in a similar fashion to how a flower rises up from the ground or vision rises up from the deep halls of the mind when one is placed in a sensory deprivation chamber. I believe this to be why many people and cultures over time have said that, in the moment of inspiration, the artist is visited or inhabited by a muse or genius. They understood the notion of being swept up and away by something that they presumed outside themselves. I, however, feel that what sweeps us away is not outside ourselves but *is* ourselves, is the deepest expression of what moves in us that moves in all things and that ties us inexplicably to the world around.

Therefore, my goal in the creative process is to somehow open myself up to that dark glance, to go deep enough into myself that I go out into the world. I am reminded now of a title of one of Joseph Campbell's books, "The Inner Reaches of Outer Space." This is much how I imagine it: if I can empty my mind of all the mental clutter and exist, even for a moment, in the deep uncertainty of existence, the deep uncertainty that exists in the gap between what one feels when gazing upon looming mountains and what one can intellectualize, if I can sit before the fire, if I can sit with the dead and look into their eyes, and write from the deepest ache that feels beyond even my center, then I can touch something real, something universal, something eternal, and the residue will be left on the page.